Holiday & Other Poems by John Davidson

John Davidson was born at Barrhead, East Renfrewshire on 11th April 1857.

In 1862 his family moved to Greenock and there he began his education at Highlanders' Academy. Davidson would now spend many years at school and the beginnings of a career in various industries before gaining employment in various schools.

By now literature was a large part of his activities and his first published work was 'Bruce, A Chronicle Play' in 1886. Four other plays quickly followed including the somewhat brilliant pantomimic 'Scaramouch in Naxos' (1889).

With his reputation gradually providing an income he was also able to explore his true medium; Verse. 'In a Music Hall and Other Poems' (1891) together with 'Fleet Street Eclogues' (1893) were ample proof that he possessed a quite rare, genuine and distinctive poetic gift.

Davidson now turned further and further towards verse. In 1894 he published his most popular volume, 'Ballads and Songs' (1894), and this was followed by a further 'Fleet Street Eclogues' (Second Series) (1896) and by 'New Ballads' (1897) and 'The Last Ballad' (1899).

As the new century dawned Davidson was hard at work on a series of 'Testaments', in which he gave definite expression to his philosophy and were published over a seven year period; 'The Testament of a Vivisector' (1901), 'The Testament of a Man Forbid' (1901), 'The Testament of an Empire Builder' (1902), and 'The Testament of John Davidson' (1908).

However, on 23rd March 1909, with his finances in ruins, the onset of cancer and profound hopelessness and clinical depression he left his house for the last time. His body was only found on September 18th by some local fishermen.

Index of Contents

I0163577

POEMS

HOLIDAY

Lithe and listen, gentlemen:
Other knight of sword or pen
Shall not, while the planets shine,
Spend a holiday like mine: —

Fate and I, we played at dice:
Thrice I won and lost the main;
Thrice I died the death, and thrice
By my will I lived again.

First, a woman broke my heart,
As a careless woman can,
Ere the aureoles depart
From the woman and the man.

Dead of love, I found a tomb
Anywhere: beneath, above,
Worms nor stars transpierced the gloom
Of the sepulchre of love.

Wine-cups were the charnel-lights;
Festal songs, the funeral dole;
Joyful ladies, gallant knights,
Comrades of my buried soul.

Tired to death of lying dead
In a common sepulchre,
On an Easter morn I sped
Upward where the world's astir.

Soon I gathered wealth and friends;
Donned the livery of the hour:
And atoning diverse ends
Bridged the gulf to place and power.

All the brilliances of Hell
Crushed by me, with honeyed breath
Fawned upon me till I fell,
By pretenders done to death.

Buried in ah outland tract,
Long I rotted in the mould,
Though the virgin woodland lacked
Nothing of the age of gold.

Roses spiced the dews and damps
Nightly falling of decay;
Dawn and sunset lit the lamps
Where entombed I deeply lay.

My Companions of the Grave
Were the flowers, the growing grass;
Larks intoned a morning stave;
Nightingales, a midnight mass.

But at me, effete and dead,
Did my spirit gibe and scoff:
Then the gravecloth from my head,
And my shroud — I shook them off!

Drawing strength and subtle craft
Out of ruin's husk and core,
Through the earth I ran a shaft
Upward to the light once more.

Soon I made me wealth and friends'
Donned the livery of the age;
And atoning many ends
Reigned as sovereign, priest, and mage.

But my pomp and towering state,
Puissance and supreme device
Crumbled on the cast of Fate —
Fate, that plays with loaded dice.

I whose arms had harried Hell
Naked faced a heavenly host:
Carved with countless wounds I fell,

Sadly yielding up the ghost.

In a burning mountain thrown
(Titans such a tomb attain)
Many a grisly age had flown
Ere I rose and lived again.

Parched and charred I lay; my cries
Shook and rent the mountain-side;
Lustres, decades, centuries
Fled while daily there I died.

But my essence and intent
Ripened in the smelting fire:
Flame became my element;
Agony, my soul's desire.

Twenty centuries of Pain,
Mightier than Love or Art,
Woke the meaning in my brain
And the purpose of my heart

Straightway then aloft I swam
Through the mountain's sulphurous sty:
Not eternal death could damn
Such a hardy soul as I.

From the mountain's burning crest
Like a god I come again,
And with an immortal zest
Challenge Fate to throw the main.

THE LAST SONG

"Songster" — say you? — "sing!"
Not a note have I!
Effort cannot bring
Fancy from the sky:
Hark! — the rusty string!
Leave me here to die.
"Songster, songster, sing!
Tune your harp and try.
Sing! we bid you sing
Once before you die!"

Withered, angry, mad,

Who would list to me,
Since my singing sad
Troubled earth and sea
When my heart was glad
And my fancy free?
"Sad or joyful, sing!
Look about, above!
Trust the world and sing
Once again of love!"

Love? I know the word:
Love is of the rose.
Have you seen or heard
Love among the snows?
Yet my heart is stirred!
Nay, my fancy glows!
"Summon all your powers;
Sing of joy or woe —
Love among the flowers,
Love amidst the snow."

Death is but a trance:
Life, but now begun!
Welcome change and chance:
Though my days are done,
Let the planets dance
Lightly round the sun!
Morn and evening clasp
Earth with loving hands —
In a ruddy grasp
All the pleasant lands!

Now I hear the deep
Bourdon of the bee,
Like a sound asleep
Wandering o'er the lea;
While the song-birds keep
Urging nature's plea.
Hark! the violets pray
Swooning in the sun!

Hush! the roses say
Love and death are one!

Loud my dying rhyme
Like a trumpet rings;
Love in death sublime
Soars on sovran wings,

While the world and time
Fade like shadowy things.
"Love upon his lip
Hovers loath to part;
Death's benignant grip
Fastens on his heart."

Look, a victor hies
Bloody from the fight,
And a woman's eyes
Greet him in the night —
Softly from the skies
Like sidereal light!
"Love is all in all,
Life and death are great.
Bring a purple pall;
Bury him in state."

A RUNNABLE STAG

When the pods went pop on the broom, green broom,
And apples began to be golden-skinned,
We harboured a stag in the Priory coomb,
And we feathered his trail up-wind, up-wind,
We feathered his trail up-wind —
A stag of warrant, a stag, a stag,
A runnable stag, a kingly crop,
Brow, bay and tray and three on top,
A stag, a runnable stag.

Then the huntsman's horn rang yap, yap, yap,
And "Forwards" we heard the harbourer shout;
But 'twas only a brocket that broke a gap
In the beechen underwood, driven out,
From the underwood antlered out
By warrant and might of the stag, the stag,
The runnable stag, whose lordly mind
Was bent on sleep, though beamed and tined
He stood, a runnable stag.

So we tufted the covert till afternoon
With Tinkerman's Pup and Bell-of-the-North;
And hunters were sulky and hounds out of tune
Before we tufted the right stag forth,
Before we tufted him forth,
The stag of warrant, the wily stag,

The runnable stag with his kingly crop,
Brow, bay and tray and three on top,
The royal and runnable stag.

It was Bell-of-the-North and Tinkerman's Pup,
That stuck to the scent till the copse was drawn.
"Tally ho! tally ho!" and the hunt was up,
The tufters whipped and the pack laid on,
The resolute pack laid on,
And the stag of warrant away at last,
The runnable stag, the same, the same,
His hoofs on fire, his horns like flame,
A stag, a runnable stag.

"Let your gelding be: if you check or chide
He stumbles at once and you're out of the hunt;
For three hundred gentlemen, able to ride,
On hunters accustomed to bear the brunt,
Accustomed to bear the brunt,
Are after the runnable stag, the stag,
The runnable stag with his kingly crop,
Brow, bay and tray and three on top,
The right, the runnable stag."

By perilous paths in coomb and dell,
The heather, the rocks, and the river-bed,
The pace grew hot, for the scent lay well,
And a runnable stag goes right ahead,
The quarry went right ahead —
Ahead, ahead, and fast and far;
His antlered crest, his cloven hoof,
Brow, bay and tray and three aloof,
The stag, the runnable stag.

For a matter of twenty miles and more,
By the densest hedge and the highest wall,
Through herds of bullocks he baffled the lore
Of harbourer, huntsman, hounds and all,
Of harbourer hounds and all —
The stag of warrant, the wily stag,
For twenty miles, and five and five,
He ran, and he never was caught alive,
This stag, this runnable stag.

When he turned at bay in the leafy gloom,
In the emerald gloom where the brook ran deep,
He heard in the distance the rollers boom,
And he saw in a vision of peaceful sleep,

In a wonderful vision of sleep,
A stag of warrant, a stag, a stag,
A runnable stag in a jewelled bed,
Under the sheltering ocean dead,
A stag, a runnable stag.

So a fateful hope lit up his eye,
And he opened his nostrils wide again,
And he tossed his branching antlers high
As he headed the hunt down the Charlock glen,
As he raced down the echoing glen
For five miles more, the stag, the stag,
For twenty miles, and five and five,
Not to be caught now, dead or alive,
The stag, the runnable stag.

Three hundred gentlemen, able to ride,
Three hundred horses as gallant and free,
Beheld him escape on the evening tide,
Far out till he sank in the Severn Sea,
Till he sank in the depths of the sea —
The stag, the buoyant stag, the stag
That slept at last in a jewelled bed
Under the sheltering ocean spread,
The stag, the runnable stag.

MERRY ENGLAND

Island-Kingdom, our island-state,
Merry England, where fancy dwells
In pageant, pilgrimage, high debate,
And sprightly music of morris-bells;
Tourneys for love and battles for hate;
Torches, garlands, exultant bells —
Challenging trumpets and festal bells;
Wars of the Roses, land-locked strife,
World-wide wars with France and Spain:
The colour and pulse of that gallant life —
Shall we never recover the mood again?

Rhythmic deeds, melodious words: —
Merry England, the heart of mirth: —
Songs of lovers and songs of birds;
A bell for death and a bell for birth —
Jubilant fifths and sombre thirds:
Pessimist? Optimist? — death and birth!

Englishmen only on English earth!
Confident daring, travail and strife,
Battle and storm on the Spanish Main —
How shall the fancy that donned that life
Be decked and renewed with such pride again?

England's fancy shall live again —
Merry England across the seas! —
Jewelled with isles of the Spanish Main,
Gifts of the opulent destinies:
England's heart and England's brain,
Throbbing and thinking in many seas
Belov'd of the opulent destinies.
Bluebird, oriole, bobolink,
Hark to them, hear them how they sing,
Where England's Canadians work and think,
Woo and wed in the throng of Spring!

Axes ring on the mountain-sides —
England's gain from England's loss! —
Lonely at night the ranchman rides,
Humming a tune to the Southern Cross;
Argosies on Austral tides,
From Charles's Wain to the Southern Cross,
Barter the Plough for the Southern Cross!
Lord! how the English hew their way,
Courage and fortune leading the van!
Round the world with the break of day,
Room for him, room for the Englishman!

Saxon, Norman, Dansker, Celt —
Merry England, mother of mirth! —
Gird the earth with an English belt,
Englishmen all to the ends of the earth!
Gold and grain on Rand and Veldt,
Orchards, harvests over the earth —
Liners and merchantmen round the earth;.
Power from East to Western Ind,
Power and pomp on the Indian Main,
And wonder with every whispering wind
To dip our dreams in the dew again.

England, decked and dowered by fate —
Room for England, so please you room!
Sea-Kings' realm, our Ocean-state,
Woven upon the world's wide loom;
Dyed and tried in high debate,
And ever renewed on the world's wide loom,

With weaving fleets in a world-wide loom —
Warp and woof of the sea's wide loom:
Shall garnish fancy in every land
With rhythmic deed and delight again —
Merry England from strand to strand,
From the Spanish Main to the Indian Main.

LABURNUM AND LILAC

Where the New River strays,
Eddying in olive green
And chrysophrase,
And briefly seen
In traffic-troubled ways,
Laburnum showers
Its verdant gold,
Its clustered flowers
Instilled and scrolled
With emerald sap:
Green-tinted gold
In April's lap
Unpursed, unrolled;
A mint of flowers,
A hoard untold,
Laburnine showers
Of greenish gold.

Like ostrich plumes
The jolly donahs wear,
Light-tressed or dark,
The lilac blooms
In every park and square
And blooms in Finsbury Park;
Or heliotrope or mauve,
Snowy or dark,
The lilac blooms
In white and purple plumes.

"What? Russell Square!"
There's lilac there!
And Torrington
And Woburn Square
Intrepid don
The season's wear.
In Gordon Square and Euston Square —
There's lilac, there's laburnum there!

In green and gold and lavender
Queen Square and Bedford Square,
All Bloomsbury and all Soho
With every sunbeam gayer grow,
Greener grow and gayer.

The lindens in the Mall
Resound with bees;
The plane-trees shed their bark —
The eager trees
That promptly grow so tall;
And in St. James's Park
Full-throated chant
The song-thrush and the merle
Till dusk forbids,
And dim-eyed night encamps
Where now the chestnuts vaunt
Their leafy pyramids
And lustrous lamps
Of ruby, gold, and pearl;
But in St. James's shade
Of elms antique,
The mystic porch
Of Nature's bridal-room
That coupled songsters seek,
The lilac swings a censer
Of ravishing perfume,
And rich laburnums braid
The green-gilt gloom
With flame intenser
Than the chestnut's torch.

APPLE-TREES

When autumn stains and dapples
The diverse land,
Thickly studded with apples
The apple-trees stand.

Their mystery none discovers,
So none can tell —
Not the most passionate lovers
Of garth and fell;
For the silent sunlight weaves
The orchard spell,
Bough, bole, and root,

Mysterious, hung with leaves,
Embossed with fruit.

Though merle and throstle were loud,
Silent their passion in spring,
A blush of blossom wild-scented;
And now when no song-birds sing,
They are heavy with apples and proud
And supremely contented —
All fertile and green and sappy,
No wish denied,
Exceedingly quiet and happy
And satisfied!

No jealousy, anger, or fashion
Of strife
Perturbs in their stations
The apple-trees. Life
Is an effortless passion,
Fruit, bough, and stem,
A beautiful patience
For them.

Frost of the harvest-moon
Changes their sap to wine;
Ruddy and golden soon
Their clustered orbs will shine,
By favour
Of many a wind,
Of morn and noon and night,
Fulfilled from core to rind
With savour
Of all delight

NOVEMBER

I

Regents Park

Poplars, ashes, flaunting wreaths of June
Green among the tarnished oaks, outstayed
Lindens, plane-trees, chestnuts, elms so soon
Ragged, draggle-tailed, or stripped and flayed.

Somnolent canal and urban wold,

Lawn and lake with saffron leaves and red,
Crimson leaves and olive, brown and gold,
Bronze and topaz leaves engarlanded,

Underneath the feet of winter flung —
Cloth of Bagdad richer than the stuft
Woven in Tyrian looms, by poets sung
Barbarous when the world was young enough

Frankly to adore a purple stain —
Graced the season mantled in its breath
Glittering pale, or draped in swarthy rain,
Victor in decay and peer of death.

II

The Enfield Road

Capitalled and coped with massive cloud,
Lofty elms, a wayside colonnade,
Shaft or bole erect and interboughed,
Forestward, a beckoning passage made.

Like a golden haze, a misty veil
Diapered with sequins, foliage lined
All the vista, yellow discs and frail
Stalks that snapped against the chariest wind.

Flapping rooks alit on blighted sheaves;
Ruddy haws in ragged hedges glowed;
Elfin companies of withered leaves
Pattered nowhere down the sodden road.

Sullen in the west across the floor
Swept and garnished of the wintry plain,
Sunset smouldered like a furnace-door
Black and shot with cramoisie in grain.

III

Epping Forest

Woods and coppices by tempest lashed;
Pollard shockheads glaring in the rain;

Jet-black underwood with crimson splashed —
Rich November, one wet crimson stain!

Turf that whispered moistly to the tread;
Bursts of laughter from the shuffled leaves;
Pools of light in distant arbours spread;
Depths of darkness under forest eaves.

High above the wind the clouds at rest
Emptied every vat and steeply hurled
Reservoirs and floods; the wild nor*west
Raked the downpour ere it reached the world;

Part in wanton sport and part in ire,
Flights of rain on ruddy foliage rang:
Woven showers like sheets of silver fire
Streamed; and all the forest rocked and sang.

IV

Box Hill

Brilliant month by legend slandered so!
Down in Surrey in the shining air
Mid-November saw the woodland grow
Green as summer still, and still as fair:

Elms perhaps, and fragrant limes forlorn
Drooped a branch, yet half I thought to hear
Men and swift machines among the corn,
Voices and the ringing harvest-gear.

Sunset saw I from the sinuous height
Box Hill rears on sombre Mulla's bank:
Darker and more dark the ruby light
Over Polsdon Arbour dying sank;

But or ever Time's nocturnal seal
Fixed the doom of day, the mid-moon's power
Did in star-attended state repeal
Darkness and the sentence of the hour.

V

Deep delight in volume, sound, and mass,
Shadow, colour, movement, multitudes,
Murmurs, cries, the traffic's rolling bass —
Subtle city of a thousand moods!

Distance, rumour, mystery, things that count,
Bravely in the memory scored and limned!
Sunset, welling like a crimson fount
Underneath the Marble Arch, o'erbrimm'd

All the smoky west. In Oxford Street
Lamps, like jewels fallen by the way
While the sun upon his urban beat
Bore the lofty burden of the day,

Magnified their offices and grew
Vital and a rosary of light,
Wreathing life that gathered heart anew
Hungry for the pleasure of the night.

Trees of winter's nakedness aware
Gleamed and disappeared like things afraid,
Dryads of the terrace and the square,
Silvery in the shadow and the shade.

Swarthy-purple creepers draped the high
Houses; leaves in elm-tree tops astir
Blurred like flakes of soot the darkling sky,
Lit with faded light of lavender.

VI

The Chilterns

I remember once a glorious thing
Crowned the season in my wandering time.
Through the year I went from earliest Spring
Hither, thither, weaving prose and rhyme,

Like a gleeman of the former age.
Sound and colour were my pensioners;
Constant on my passionate pilgrimage
Love attended me, and friends of hers,

Life and Death besides. But one day, late
Roaming in the Chilterns, want of will
Irked me, and the impotence of Fate —
Something lacking in the World, until

Bluff November in the coppice near
Loud on orient horns an onset wound,
While the larks that through the golden year
Garlanded the air with dazzling sound,

Surged upon the tempest's deafening cry —
Crests of foam about the ocean driven,
Lightning scribbled on a thund'rous sky,
Tongues of flame upon the top of heaven!

YULETIDE

Now wheel and hoof and horn
In every street
Stunned to its chimney-tops,
In every murky street —
Each lamp-lit gorge by traffic rent
Asunder,
Ravines of serried shops
By business tempests torn —
In every echoing street,
From early morn
Till jaded night falls dead,
Wheel, hoof, and horn
Tumultuous thunder
Beat
Under
A noteless firmament
Of lead.

When the winds list
A fallen cloud
Where yellow dregs of light
Befouled remain,
The woven gloom
Of smoke and mist,
The soot-entangled rain
That jumbles day and night
In city and town,
An umber-emerald shroud
Rehearsing doom,

The London fog comes down.
But sometimes silken beams,
As bright
As adamant on fire,
Of the uplifted sun's august attire,
With frosty fibrous light
Magnetic shine
On happier dreams
That abrogate despair,
When all the sparkling air
Of smoke and sulphur shriven,
Like an iced wine
Fills the high cup
Of heaven;
For urban park and lawn,
The city's scenery,
Heaths, commons, dells
That compass London rich
In greenery,
With diamond-dust of rime
Empowdered, flash
At dawn;
And tossing bells
Of stealthy hansoms chime
With silvery crash
In radiant ways
Attuned and frozen up
To concert pitch —
In resonant ways,
Where wheels and hoofs inwrought,
Cars, omnibuses, wains,
Beat, boom, and clash
Discordant fugal strains
Of cymbals, trumpets, drums;
While careless to arrive,
The nerved pedestrian comes
Exulting in the splendour overhead,
And in the live
Elastic ground,
The pavement, tense and taut,
That yields a twangling sound
At every tread.

ECLOGUES

THE IDES OF MARCH

Percy, Herbert, Basil, Ninian, Sandy

Percy
Where the brimming freshets rush
And the pebbles chafe and ring,
The leafless alders flush
With purple of the Spring.

Herbert
And the crimson osiers burn
With spathes that swell and split,
And every bract an urn
With twinkling catkins lit.

Basil
Where chaos spreads unkempt,
And formless being roves,
I wandered lost
Until I crossed
The ultramundane groves,
And dreamt last night, as Caesar dreamt,
I placed my hand in Jove's.

Ninian
And music sighed and sang,
And voices uttered doom,
And Mars's armour rang
Untouched in Caesar's room.
Most ominous of woe,
A wondering slave appeared,
Whose fingers flamed below —

Sandy
A candelabrum weird!

Ninian
Titanic beings fought,
In fiery arms on high;
The Universe was wrought
To tragic sympathy;
Nor can the years dispel
The awe of that; nor can
The tongues of poets tell
The deed these signs foreran,
For on the morrow fell
The greatest man.

Basil
What cry? what whispered word?

Percy
What music wild and sweet?

Herbert
The listening air is stirred.

Sandy
The sounds are in the street.

Basil
I hear a murmuring flood.

Percy
I hear a trembling string.

Ninian
The sounds are in our blood.

Basil
The sounds are of the Spring.

Herbert
The throstle in the brake,
Alone, and hid away,
Beginning to rehearse
His long-considered lay,
Because the blossoms wake
On the elms, the first in flower,
Repeats a broken verse
And tunes it by the hour.

Percy
And his cousin thinks him a dunce,
The blackbird, he who sings
At the top of his voice at once
While the startled woodland rings:
He peals his splendid song
Loud and fluent and clear,
For echo to prolong
And all the world to hear.

Herbert
Now like a golden gong;
Now like a crystal sphere.

Percy
For echo to prolong
And all the world to hear.

Basil
What sound is this that comes
At sunset lowly pitched?
The roll of elfin drums
Or song of things bewitched?
Perhaps the nightwind strums
The wires, with news enriched
Of peace, and silent drums —
With happy news enriched
Of silent, sleeping drums,
With war no more bewitched.

Ninian
At least the springtime comes;
For I hear in a valley I know
A sound of elfin drums,
And a shadowy clarion blow,
As the crimson threads and thrums
In the twilight sky decay,
And the wandering beetle hums
The threnody of day.

Sandy
When the spacious darkness comes,
And the crimson lights decay,
The ponderous beetle hums
The threnody of day.

Herbert
The nightwind sighs and sings.

Percy
The darkness deepening comes.

Basil
The antique curfew rings
To the roll of elfin drums.

Ninian
The flickering threads and thrums,
The ruddy brands decay;
And the mournful beetle hums
The threnody of day.

Basil
But soon the wakening comes,
And darkness dies forlorn;
And the thunder of the drums
Of the March wind ushers morn.

Ninian
And woes that wound the sight,
And spectres disappear.

Percy
And men are men of might.

Herbert
And love is crystal-clear.

Sandy
And I swear by the light,
And the noon and the night,
It is good, it is good to be here!

II

ST. MARK'S EVE

Basil, Ninian, Vivian

Basil
Late, Vivian! Midnight stirs
In the placid bosom of Time.

Vivian
I have been in the wildwood, sirs,
In the snare of a sovran rhyme;
Where blossoms and feathers and furs
Grow rich as a dazzling rhyme —
With stains of a fragrant rhyme;
And the very spathes and spurs
Are tuned to the deafening chime
Of the larks and the courage that stirs
In the heart of the vernal prime.

Ninian
In the wildwood? Here or beyond?
At home in the world or afar?
Where the bracken unfurls a frond,

Or a nebula loosens a star —
Where the fern delivers a frond,
Or a nebula utters a star?

Vivian
At home. In this hermit-nook
Of conscious pleasure and pain
I journeyed to listen and look —
With wonder to listen and look
In the Warren and Honey Lane,
By the Quicks and the Cuckoo brook
From Epping to Chingford Plain.
Where the passion of Nature stirs
Undisciplined, up and down
I wandered the wildwood, sirs,
On the margin of London town —
In the forest that's ours and hers
On the threshold of London town.

Ninian
Did you see then the blackthorn blaze
Against the empurpled glow
Of the glades and the woodland ways?
Did the violet forest glow
Where the budded leaf delays,
And chaplets pallid as snow
On the twisted blackthorn blaze —
Coronals, garlands, sprays
Like fresh, moon-silvered snow?

Basil
Did you hear from Highbeach tower
The mellow quarter-chime —
From the belfry of Highbeach tower
Did you hear the music of Time,
Like silken banners unfurled?
From the ancient and hallowed bower
Of the virginal bride of the world,
Did you hear the melodious hour
Like broidered banners unfurled —
With the dulcet and virginal power
Of Time, the bride of the world?

Vivian
I saw the blackthorn blaze
Like wreaths of moonlit snow,
Where the budded leaf delays
And the violet woodlands glow;

From Highbeach steepled tower
I heard the quarter-chime —
From the ancient and hallowed bower
Of the beautiful virgin, Time,
I heard the melodious vesper hour
And the sprightly quarter-chime.
Then the blackbird finished his song
On a penetrant, resolute note;
Though the thrush descanted long,
For he knows no tune by rote —
With sighs descanted long
Of the sorrow he aches to tell;
With sobs and shuddering moans,
Like one that sings in Hell,
He laced the phantom over-tones
Of the mellow vesper-bell:
Some terror he fain would tell,
But he never can strike the note:
So the thrush descanted long,
While the blackbird finished his song.
And the woodwele's laughter ceased
In his ash-green gurgling throat
On the fringe of the tones released
By the vibrant vesper-bell —
The forest laughter ceased
In the wake of the twilight bell,
And high, so high, from the dusky sky
The last lark breathless fell.
But the nightingales sang on
Like welling founts of sound,
As the saffron sunset paler shone
And the darkness grew profound;
The nightingales sang on
And the sleepless cuckoos beat
Their dulcimers anon, anon,
In the echoing woodland street —
Their golden dulcimers anon
In every forest street.
And lo! from their secret bowers
In the shadowy depths of the chace,
With lanterns jewelled like flowers
In state at a stately pace —
The elfin-folk from their hallowed bowers
In the innermost shrine of the chace,
Came, swinging their fragrant and luminous flowers,
To dance in the market-place —
Came with their dances and lanterned flowers
To the forest's market-place.

And I watched them dancing for hours
In elfin pomp and state:
I saw the elves and I watched them for hours,
And therefore I come so late.

Basil
How say you? An April tale
Of the nightingale's song and the lark's;
Or a vision at best, or a dream?

Ninian
Nay, for enchantments prevail,
And things are as strange as they seem.
At the mystical Tide of St. Mark's
A pregnant fantasy stirs,
And prodigies happen o nights.

Vivian
And I saw them, I saw them, sirs —
The elves in their woodland rites!
When the vesper-bell had rung,
And the last lark dropped from the sky;
When the cuckoo's golden tongue,
And the nightingale's rhapsody
Full-filled the forest with sound,
From their secret and hallowed bowers
In the woodland depths profound,
From the innermost heart of the chace,
The elves with their lanterned flowers
Trooped forth at an elfin pace;
And I watched them dancing for hours
In the forest's market-place.

III

THE TWENTY-FOURTH OF MAY

Basil, Ninian, Brian, Vivian, Lionel

Brian
Must this be Empire-Day?

Basil
The date is fixed.

Brian

Forfend
The omen, powers on high

Basil
Shame, traitor, shame! Amend
So treasonous a sigh.
Empire and Empire-Day —

Brian
I still mistrust them, I! —

Basil
Have come and come to stay!

Brian
I hate the name, the thing!
You know the prophets say,
"Empire begins the end:
The loves, the hopes we sing,
Our sweetest common good
Will fade, their source decay,
And fancy's naive device
Unmourned depart away —
Art and our freer mood
For ever and a day."
So stiff is empire's price,
The penalty of power.

Ninian
But the drama of the woods,
That deepens every hour,
No change in men can change,
While the murmuring cushat broods,
And the restless fern-owls range
The night-winds interstrown
With wonders, jewelled wings
Of moths and chafers — sown
With silken singing wings
Of lost nocturnal things.

Lionel
Not fear, not love, not hate,
Not shame, not wounded pride
Can heighten or abate
The jocund summer-tide
That blossoms hour by hour —
The surf and crested tide
Of the fragrant hawthorn flower.

Vivian

No human joy or care,
Not envy, age, or pain,
Not the whole world's despair
Can tarnish, taint, or stain
One gold-bossed silver shield
Of the daisies of the field —
The land-wide Milky Way
Of the myriad eyes of day.

Brian

To me the amber studs
Of the kingcups on the leas,
And the fragrant hawthorn buds
Are but the earth's disease;
And the daisies in the grass
A snowy leprosy.

Basil

Hush, slanderer, hush! Alas,
How deep your discontent!

Brian

Imperial thoughts for me
Decolour and unscent
The violet and the rose;
For empire is the womb
Qf teeming wars and woes,
The enemy of chance
That keeps the world in hope,
And the murderer and the tomb
Of art and all romance.

Basil

If that's the only ill,
The source of all your gloom,
No longer need you mope.
Such dire imperial doom
Has been, and shadows still
All landlocked empire, shut
In one unhealthy room;
A drilled mechanic state
That jolts in one deep rut —
Whose grave, or soon or late,
Is its habitual rut,
By time and chance and fate
For ever sealed and shut.

Brian
Infallible rebuke
That shames imperial pride!

Basil
The doom that overtook
The empires of the past;
The doom that must betide
All rule however fast
Enfeoffed with power and law,
That makes its interest, first and last,
To hold the world in awe.
But England's Ocean-state
Enthroned upon the sea,
The armed and equal mate
Of power and liberty,
Has this for doom and fate —
To set the peoples free.

Lionel
Nobler than empire — word
Ill-omened, out of date! —
What name shall be conferred
On England's Ocean-state?

Basil
We need no other name;
Our origin, our fate,
Our history speaks, our fame,
In England's Ocean-state.

Vivian
Wherever England comes
The lowliest has his chance.

Lionel
Our English story sums
The meaning of Romance.

Basil
We bid the poet drink
Till Hippocrene be dry,
And the thinker dare to think
The sun out of the sky.

Lionel
We bid the dreamer, drunk

With dreaming, dream again;
And fakir, mollah, monk
To any heaven attain.

Basil
Then though these isles were sunk
And buried in the sea,
Our England would remain
Wherever men are free.

Ninian
Embattled usage falls
At the beating of our drums;
All proud originals
Have scope where England comes.

Vivian
As free as birds that sing
And serenade the morn.

Lionel
As the swallow on the wing,
Or the blackbird on the thorn.

Basil
Or the throstle, purged of scorn
For the music in his heart —
That takes such loving pains
To school his angry heart,
And now at last attains
The mastery of his art.

IV

BAPTIST TIDE

Basil, Lionel, Brian, Menzies

Basil
Outcast and vagrant, hail!
Unhappy, wandering star,
You sojourn here, unchid;
We love you — as you are,
Rejected, scorned, forbid,
Targe of the world's abuse.

Lionel

What nectar, dark or pale,
To drink your happier cheer in?
What brew, what auburn ale,
What blood, what golden juice
Of Albany or Erin?

Menzies

The grape, the grape: no malt
To deaden soul and sense.
Let some illustrious wine
My heart and brain exalt,
And crowded opulence
Of fantasy be mine.

Basil

Your brain shall teem with sights
Desirable as youth;
And sense and soul divide
The ravished world between them.

Brian

Bethink you, sirs: in sooth
We should be Nazarites,
For this is Baptist Tide.

Lionel

Let formalists demean them
As ancient modes provide:
We take no oath, no vow;
Nor shall our hearts abide
In bondage of the past.

Basil

The adolescent world
Is but beginning now;
And men are men at last.

Brian

Yet the sweet heaven unfurled
About us like a rose,
Nor ending, nor beginning,
Nor age, nor ailment knows.

Lionel

Though that were certain, folk
Who cannot make an end
Of simple-hearted sinning,

Who have their lives to spend,
And must endure the yoke
Of human joys and woes,
Seek still a new beginning,
Desire a sweeter song,
Expect the compassed close
Of misery and wrong.

Basil
A cup of wine can change
Despair to deep delight.

Brian
An overture that jars
Upon our mood! We range
The purlieus of the night
On thoughts that seek the stars;
You drag us down to earth,
And urge a vinous mirth!

Basil
Nay, now; fill, drink, and mark: —
A Burgundy mature;
Romance Conti, dark
As carmine jewels, pure
As Cdte d'Or's golden noons,
And spiced with dewy scent
Of rich autumnal moons.

Brian
A wine whose virtue's spent
Before the lees appear!

Basil
By Dionysius, no!
A mystery slumbers here,
A rite, a sacrament,
Whose nature I can show.
We drink material power;
The inmost soul of wine
Is adamant, the flower
Of carbon: light and heat
Long-hoarded in the mine;
Mettle of bread and meat;
The dawn whose crimson flood
Intoxicates the east;
The tissue and the heart
Of organism; the blood,

The seed of man and beast
Become by Nature's art
Sterile as candent flame,
And yet the stuff, the breath
Of noble strife, of fame,
Of myths that folk invent
To give the past a name;
Ethereal life in death,
Potable ravishment.

Lionel
The naked facts; the truth;
The power, the poetry!

Basil
Now will our outcast see
Some vision of his youth;
Of summer's flower and leaf,
Of emprise meetly done;
A happy gleaner's sheaf,
Or love, or battle won;
Some joy beyond belief:
For he has drunk the sun,
Drunk up the night and day,
Drunk down the dregs of grief,
And drunk the world away.

Lionel
He sees us not, nor hears;
A glory fills his eyes,
Like one through crystal tears
Beholding Paradise.

Menzies
Not rubies set in gold
Of matchless flame and worth,
But dawn and sunset scrolled
About the emerald earth!
Oh, moon of my desire,
Bend from your heaven above,
A lily sweet, on fire
With newly budded love!
Bend from your heaven; be mine
Once more before I die,
And let life's hallowed wine
Empurple earth and sky
In hyacinthine hours,
And dusky midnights hung

With stars and passion-flowers
And ecstasies unsung!

Lionel
Entranced into the street
He wanders like a shade!

Brian
He treads on wingfed feet:
I think his grave is made!

Basil
His soul is bathed in light,
His heart for love athirst:
Were he to die to-night
I scarce should call him curst.

V

THE FEAST OF ST. MARTHA

Basil, Lionel, Vivian, Brian

Brian,
Perturbed by wealth, perturbed by want,
With angered brain and breaking heart,
Why will the world the market haunt?
If folk would choose the better part!

Lionel
Folk must be troubled; work and think;
Devote their strength; exhaust their health.
I love St. Martha, meat and drink,
Labour and thrift, and skill and wealth.

Vivian
If exorcism avail not, leave
The phantom woes you sorrow for.

Brian
No phantoms; facts: for facts I grieve,
Authentic things that dreams abhor: —
Imprisoned clouds that spin and weave
Complex machinery of war
(Torpedoes, cannon, latent rage
Impounding peace) as easily

As happy playmates knit a cage
Of rushes for a butterfly.

Lionel
And chastened lightning, pick and choice
Of all man's wonder-working might,
A public scribe, an airy voice,
The dazzling conqueror of the night!

Basil
To whisper over heath and holt,
To herald tidings everywhere,
To travel on a thunder-bolt
By land, or sea, or middle air!

Vivian
The docile lightning! Jupiter,
Could no foreboding Proteus see
Your armament celestial wear
The livery of humanity!

Brian
Miraculous; but watch them work —
Steam, electricity: behold
Iniquity and rapine lurk
Where'er machinery forges gold!

Basil
I grant the worst: the piston-rod
Undoes the handicraftsman, seals
The doom of labour; clad and shod
In unseen lightning, business steals
The garnered wealth of rank and power,
The frugal means of proud content,
The widow's mite, the orphan's dower,
The toiler's hard-earned increment.

Lionel
And thus the promise darkly given
Fulfils itself: a child can tell
In Rich-and-Poor an actual Heaven
Deep-rooted in an actual Hell!

Vivian
Unhallowed jest! But let me laugh!
By all the powers without a doubt
The railway and the telegraph
Have brought millennium about!

Brian
Oh, shame! That one man may be great
And loll at ease, a god on high,
Beneath, the castings of his fate,
A myriad outworn workers sigh.

Basil
But how if that be just? Aha!
The thing is so; therefore must be.
Skilled and unskilled automata
Would all escape from slavery.
Whoever grasps what all esteem,
What all desire, wealth, power, renown,
Conceives and dares while others dream;
And he who wins, deserves the crown.

Brian
Usurious contracts, lawless gains
That fill the workhouse, stock the haunts
Of vice?

Basil
The great world's growing pains
Whose hardy soul no evil daunts!

Lionel
This very lightning you decry —

Brian
Ame damnée by the broker's hearth!
Promoter's tout, exploiter's spy! —

Lionel
Is yet the angel of the earth.
Not long shall men abuse the sons
Of men; the tyrant's doom was signed
When lightning learned to rouse at once
The righteous wrath of all mankind.

Basil
The earth itself is now inspired!

Vivian
It knows delight, it feels distress!

Lionel
Ten thousand wires and nerves unwired

Have given the globe self-consciousness!

Basil
Why brood and muse on sordid scenes,
Why pick and point at faults and flaws?
Ignore uncertain ways and means;
Regard alone the final cause.

Brian
Who can declare why man was made?

Basil
The lover knows, the children guess;
War, study, pastime, toil and trade
Have one sole purpose, Happiness.

Vivian
Only decaying types incur
Remorse and moral misery!
Were I a great philosopher
This should my metaphysic be,
A mighty Will to Happiness.

Lionel
Therefore it is the earth is round
And speeds through Heaven, a globe express
For infinite Elysium bound!

Vivian
Therefore the orbs that rule the year
Establish seasonable times,
And deck our well-appointed sphere
In purfled robes of diverse climes.

Lionel
Love therefore sighs with fragrant breath
For loftier heavens and songs unsung.

Basil
And therefore shall benignant death
Maintain the world for ever young.

Lionel
Therefore were women made divine,
With beauty, purpose, power to bless
The overloaded masculine
Incarnate Will to Happiness.

Vivian
Therefore the all-embracing sea
Doth with tempestuous voice demand,
"What power shall keep the golden key
That opes the gate of every land?"

Brian
Therefore we torture heart and brain,
And cherish neither life nor health!
We tax the past, the future drain —

Basil
In our divine desire for wealth.
We must be rich: for whom should gold
Be meant if not for you and me?
In every age the wise and bold
Have gathered treasure ardently.

Lionel
A health to England's golden rose,
Her affluence of material stuff!

Vivian
A health to all the rich and those
Who never can be rich enough!

Basil
And health to England's thrifty sons
And thrifty daughters; health to all
Courageous, battling, troubled ones
Who keep St. Martha's Festival.

VI

BARTLEMAS

Basil, Lionel, Vivian

Lionel
From an obsolete, festival mood —
(Ere the people grew wise and aware,
Transcending the bad and the good.
How extinct was the Fun of the Fair) —
Out of Smithfield with vapours endued
Of the rank Babylonian lair,
Where Mirth and her fatherless brood

Carouse it in Bartlemy Fair,
I come, by the mass, by the rood,
From the crusted, old Fun of the Fair!

Vivian
From the Forest I come whereabout
The silences, harvested, throng —
Autumnal the silences throng:
No throstle, no blackbird devout
As the seraphim mingle their song,
With perfume entangle the light
And powder the woodland with pearl,
Nor usher the star-stricken night
With incense and melody rare;
The song-thrush devout and the merle
No longer enrapture the air
With concord of ruby and pearl.

Basil
Then you of the Forest shall spin
A tissue of rhythmical words —
Of jewelled, diaphanous words;
And he shall delight in the din
Of Smithfield and Bartlemas Birds —
In the venial, carnival sin
Of Bartholomew's roystering Birds;
While I as a guerdon prepare
In our mazer of maple that held
The hydromel, quaffed at the Fair
And older than scriptural eld:
As wassail and guerdon supply,
From a formula ancient as eld
A nectar to drink of and die,
In our mazer of maple, that held
The hydromel quaffed at the Fair
Ere the people grew wise and aware.

Vivian
Alack that the truth must be told!
Not once now their dulcimers sweet,
That haunted the Forest of old,
The cuckoos, predominant, beat;
Their echoing pastoral, tolled
In every o'er-canopied street
On dulcimers, dulcet as gold,
Not now will the cuckoos repeat;
Reverberant cantos unrolled,
A thunder of dulcimers sweet,

Through the flower-writhen Forest of old
No longer the cuckoos repeat.

Lionel
But yesterday rose on the air,
With the odour of burning entwined,
The breath of an agonised prayer —
But yesterday, braiding the wind
With an incense, nor holy, nor rare
When they tortured the flesh and the mind —
The body as well as the mind;
When the learned and the lewd had to die
For the rights of the tongue and the pen,
And martyrdom shrouded the sky
In the smoke of the burning of men;
Where now in the shouldering press
Of the stareabouts destined to stare,
By the booths and the stalls in the stress
Of the tide and the trough of the Fair —
In the narrows and straits of the Fair,
While the cressets, the torches, and links,
Beginning to blossom and flare
As the sun in the Occident sinks
With phantoms embroider the air —
While the cressets and vaporous links,
As the sun that transfigured the Fair
In his western brazier sinks,
With witchcraft impregnate the air,
Arises the mercantile cry
As of souls in the depths of despair —
Of a people at home with despair,
"What lack you and what will you buy?"
The challenge and lure of the Fair!
"What lack you, sirs? Buy, will you buy?
Ripe costard or Catherine pear?
Is it hey for the lust of the eye?
Will you trip it, coranto or jig?
But first you must eat or you die,
Of a hallowed Bartholomew pig —
Of a savoury Bartlemas pig!"
Then hey for the Fun of the Fair,
The babel of noise and the cry,
The turbulent shows in the glare
Of the cressets that lacquer the sky —
That fume as they lacquer the sky!
It's ho for the Fun of the Fair!
And it's hey for the lust of the eye!
Ripe costard and Catherine pear,

And the yellow gowns fluttering by —
Green sleeves at Bartholomew Fair,
And the light of a riotous eye!

Basil
Green leaves in the Forest; green sleeves-
I modulate Lionel's cry —
At the Fair; in the Forest, green leaves,
And the glance of an innermost eye.

Vivian
No longer the nightingales chant
To the silvery pulses of night,
That echo the measure and grant
Responsal of starry delight:
No nightingales longer descant
To the stars as they throb with delight
Of the passionate answer they grant
The music that troubles the night —
As they vibrate and bloom with delight
In the hanging gardens of night.
For the silences, harvested, throng,
Though the gold and purpureal dye —
Though the lacquer, the mordant, and dye
Of the autumn, like sounds of a song
Into colour transmutable, lie
On the Forest — the crystalline tune
That the spheres were imagined to play
Into colour transformed in the noon
Of an ever adventurous day;
Above and within and about,
The perfected silences throng —
In the Forest the silences throng:
No throstle, no blackbird devout
As the seraphim mingle their song,
With perfume entangle the light
And powder the woodland with pearl,
Nor usher the star-stricken night
With incense and melody rare;
The song-thrush devout and the merle
No longer enrapture the air
With concord of ruby and pearl;
Nor now can the nightingale sing
Expecting a stellar reply;
No fugues intergarlanded ring
Of the earth and the clusters on high —
Sidereal echoes that bring
The crystalline tears and the sigh

For the end of a beautiful thing
That soldered the earth and the sky.

VII

OUR DAY

"Nelson had several times said to Captain Hardy and Dr. Scott, 'The 21st will be our day.'"
— Mahan's Life of Nelson.

Basil, **Vivian**

Basil
The chill wind whispers winter: night sets in;
And now, by many a sounding thoroughfare,
Life, like a tidal wave, begins to fill
The theatres and halls and hidden nooks,
Wherein it clangs and seethes and spends itself.

Enter **Lionel**.

And whence come you?

Vivian
From wandering to and fro
Somewhere in London — London the unknown;
Which none can ever know, none ever see,
But only wonder at and wander in!

Basil
The City of the World, ancient and proud,
Vast, thronged, and awful; richer than the floor
Of ocean and its unsacked treasure-house;
An insolent city and a beautiful;
A place of mirth and sadness infinite:
Of infinite horror, infinite despair,
Infinite courage and felicity.
What! Do we read your thoughts, your eyes that speak
Of greatnesses beheld?

Lionel
All day I saw
A greater thing than London; now at night
The ample vision looms more excellent —
The vision of a thing that shall endure
When London is as Babylon; shall shine

A jewel in eternal memory;
Shall on the summit of achievement burn,
A challenge and a beacon for the brave:
The perfect battle-pageant of the deep,
Trafalgar.

Basil
You beheld Trafalgar?

Lionel
Now!
I watch it now!

Vivian
Show us this sight of sights!
Make us behold Trafalgar and the pride
Of England, Nelson!

Lionel
Look and see; who looks
With insight, can! A fragile form,
The delicate sheath of valour absolute;
Ambition, daring, honour, constancy,
Prescience, dominion, passion, scope, design,
A woman's tenderness, an infant's awe,
An adamantine courage, mercy, power
Attuned and fateful in an invalid!
Sea-lord, sea-god, his clear, transcendent love
Endowed his friends with lustre of his own,
And saw no blemish for excess of light
Which his great spirit shed: his glittering scorn,
His hate for England's sake of England's foes,
Diviner than his love, at England's need
O'erthrew the splendid Titan who essayed
To wrest the loyal sea from English hands,
Holding in trust that greatest gift of Fate.
The Nile, the Baltic, saw his pregnant war;
The palsied navies shrivelled at his touch;
So suddenly he came, so swiftly smote,
So wholly conquered, that his deeds remain
The bulwark maritime of England's power.
Nothing could tame his soul: that ocean-hunt
About the Atlantic and about in quest
Of action France and Spain denied,
Whetted his lust of battle; long delay,
That withers enterprise and rots desire
Even of enduring things, augmented all
His purpose and matured the valiant seed

Of utmost victory. Wherefore upon the dawn
Foreknown of battle — for the Admiral said
"The twenty-first will be our day" — he paced
His quarter-gallery subtly clad already
In the shadow of his glory; prepossessed
Besides with death; and like a spirit calm
That treads the threshold of eternity.
Now, when the morning brimmed the western world,
And on the weather-gleam a headland rose
Assured of fame, and the confederate fleets
Appeared between, hull crowding hull, five miles
Of armament, our great sea-warrior bade
The battle be. Southward the ships of France,
The ships of Spain, northward the English sailed,
As if they meant to pass each other by
In some majestic ritual of the tide.
But Nelson's signals, winged like thought aloft,
Undid that minuet! Twelve sail of his,
The weather line, with Collingwood to lee,
Bore up amain — the wind west by nor'-west —
And eastward stood athwart the banded fleets,
That veered unwieldily and headed north
With safe retreat on Cadiz, till Nelson's touch
Precipitated battle — he on their van
And Collingwood against their southern flank:
Two columns opportunely; yet to the end
The sailing order held the battle-line —
Our Admiral's prophecy and inspired device.
That happy signal first: "England expects
That every man will do his duty"; then
Drums beat to quarters: gunners, stripped and girt,
The naked flesh of England against the fire
And rending bolt of England's foes, unlashed '
Their ordnance: frowning crews, equipped
With linstock, priming-iron, rammer, wad,
Crowbar and handspike, cartridge, wreaths of shot,
Stood by each carronade, each red-lipped gun;
Topman and boarder, trimmer, musketeer,
Marine and powder-boy fulfilled his post,
His deed, his errand, transfigured suddenly.
The ceremonial wind controlled the approach,
Keeping a pageant-pace; and towering sails
Of England's navy, sheeted to the sky,
Slumbered at ease, a dulcet, virgin sleep,
So placid in their bosoms the breath of heaven
Dwelt like a dream, as every vessel, groomed
For war and marshalled on the vagrant surge
Of coming tempest, rode to victory.

France fired the nuptial gun; the flags broke out
Of every nation, and the battle joined.
In front of England the Royal Sovereign first
Achieved the enemy's range. The Victory next,
Silent against a navy's broadsides, forged
Ahead; and when her double-shotted guns,
One after one, at twenty feet had ploughed
The Bucentaure endlong, aboard the doomed
Redoubtable she ran. Forthwith amid
The din of cannon against cannon, mouth
To bellowing mouth, the shriek of timber crashed
And rent, the thund'rous voice of men absorbed
In the wild trance and waking dream of war,
Carnage and agony and the rhythmic swing
And travail of the deed, as Nelson paced
His quarter-deck awaiting the superb,
Unmatched event his genius had ordained,
The fatal marksman in the enemy's top
Espied his honours and England's hero fell.
Down in the winepress of the war where blood
O'erflowed the orlop, where the wounded strewed
The noisome cockpit and the grimy sweat
Cooled on the labouring surgeons, Nelson died:
The swarthy smoke that coiled from poop to hold
Obscured the glimmering lanterns; overhead
The cannon leapt; like a taut rope the hull
Quivered from stem to stern with every shot;
And still above the thunder of the strife,
Cresting the uproar, pealed the great hurrah
Of all the English crews, as ship by ship
The baffled navies struck and Nelson's name
Became immortal.

Vivian
Such a dying deed!

Basil
So great a life, so great a death, so great
A legacy of Empire!

Lionel
All are ours,
And will be ours while Nelson's fame endures:
Great lives, great deaths for England the sea!

NEW YEAR'S EVE

Cyril, Bertram, Everard, Clarence

Cyril
The earth reposes: bird and beast
Are neutral-hued in copse and dell;
The very grass-green turf has ceased
To grow till Spring shall break the spell.

Bertram
From frozen seas the north wind blows,
From sapphire icebergs rooted deep
In Arctic fathoms.

Everard
Ancient snows
About the poles renew their sleep.

Cyril
Old continents of snow — world-old!
How comfortable there to lie
Embalmed in everlasting cold
In peace and crystal purity!

Clarence
Let these amenities increase;
But though the north be hoar with rime,
Give me the vineyard's purple peace,
The golden peace of harvest-time;
A peace with cannon frankly girt,
An armament in every sea;
A peace that wears a blood-red skirt
Deep-dyed in many a victory;
The purity of healthy lives,
Of love that sings both high and low,
Of genial husbands, happy wives,
Of mothers purer than the snow.

Cyril
Winter's a dream: the fallows feel
The hope of tilth; each blossom chaste,
Against the cold in Milan steel
Of stout hibernacle encased,
Glows with a vision of the Spring,
The fragrance and the stain of June;

And thrushes on a sudden sing
The motive of their Summer tune.

Bertram
Hush! hark! St. Paul's!

Everard
Each vibrant thought,
An orb of music, fills the ear
With rich harmonics interwrought.

Cyril
The year is dead!

Bertram
Long live the year!

Everard
Now midnight through the city rings;
A hundred reeling belfries chime,
With overtones like rhythmic strings,
The lofty madrigal of Time.

Cyril
The world speeds in a trance profound
From dark abyss to dark abyss
Across this twelve-arched bridge of sound
Between the two eternities.

Bertram
Who'll give the dreaming earth a shock,
Who set its torpid mind aglow?

Cyril
Is there an ink to etch the rock,
Ethereal lye to blanch the snow?
A cresset to contain the sun,
A crystal cup to hold the sea,
A voice to rouse the dead and done,
A highway through the galaxy?
Discover these, or things as strange,
Then shift the earth and turn the year!
Discover these, then seek to change
The mood of men, the world's career!

Clarence
There is a dish to hold the sea,
A brazier to contain the sun,

A compass for the galaxy,
A voice to wake the dead and done!

That minister of ministers,
Imagination, gathers up
The undiscovered Universe
Like jewels in a jasper cup.

Its flame can mingle north and south;
Its accent with the thunder strive;
The ruddy sentence of its mouth
Can make the ancient dead alive.

The mart of power, the fount of will
The form and mould of every star,
The source and bound of good and ill,
The key of all the things that are,

Imagination, new and strange
In every age, can turn the year,
Can shift the poles and lightly change
The mood of men, the world's career.

Cyril
What cry is this? What mad to-do?
When and by whom is this great power
That melts and forges worlds anew
Installed and used? The man, the hour?

Clarence
No other time — we understand
Nor whence, nor whither, why nor how —
Is ever at the world's command
Than this eternal present Now.

Cyril
You rede the riddle of the earth,
The ancient rule of all who ride;
And young it is as every birth,
As new and fresh as time and tide: —

By town and tower, through brake and briar,
About the world while life shall last,
Unbroken horses shod with fire
The wild-eyed moments thunder past:

Who grasps the flying mane and mounts,
Indifferent if he fail or thrive,

In happy stride with all that counts
Arrives where'er the gods arrive.

Clarence
Tis not enough to mount and ride,
No saddle, bridle, whip, nor spur;
To take the chance of time and tide,
And follow fame without demur.

I want some reason with my rhyme,
A fateful purpose when I ride;
I want to tame the steeds of Time,
To harness and command the tide:

I want a whip whose braided lash
Can echo like the crack of doom;
I want an iron mace to smash
The world and give the peoples room.

Cyril
We thought we knew you! Who are you
That talk so loud?

Clarence
One who can tell
That false is false and true is true,
Alive or dead, in Heaven or Hell.

L'ENVOI

Born, enamoured, built of fact,
Daily on destruction's brink
Venture all to put in act
Truth we trust and thought we think.

Nothing has been said or done:
Free from the forbidding past,
Knowledge only now begun
Makes an actual world at last.

Powers of Earth, of Heaven, of Hell,
Blent in us and tried and true,
By dynamic deed and spell
Forge and mould the world anew.

John Davidson was born at Barrhead, East Renfrewshire on 11th April 1857, the son of Alexander Davidson, an Evangelical Union minister and Helen née Crocket of Elgin.

In 1862 the family moved to Greenock and Davidson began his education at Highlanders' Academy. From there he began his career, aged a mere 13, at the chemical laboratory of Walker's Sugarhouse refinery. A year later he returned to Highlander's, this time as a pupil teacher.

During his later employment at the Public Analysts' Office, 1870–71 he developed a keen interest in science which later became an important characteristic of his poetry. He returned once again to the Highlander's Academy, this time for four years, in 1872, again as a pupil teacher. In 1876 he spent a year at Edinburgh University before his first scholastic employment at Alexander's Charity, Glasgow which led to short periods of employment at various other schools over the following half a dozen years.

This led to a stint at Morrison's Academy in Crieff (1885–88), and in a private school at Greenock (1888–89).

In 1885 Davidson married Margaret McArthur and the marriage produced two children, Alexander (born in 1887) and Menzies (born in 1889).

Davidson's first published work was 'Bruce, A Chronicle Play', written in the Elizabethan style, and published by a local Glasgow imprint in 1886. Four other plays quickly followed; 'Smith, A Tragic Farce' (1888), 'An Unhistorical Pastoral' (1889), 'A Romantic Farce' (1889), and then the somewhat brilliant pantomime 'Scaramouch in Naxos' (1889).

By now he was very much immersed in literature and, in 1889, he ventured to London where he frequented the famous Fleet Street pub 'Ye Olde Cheshire Cheese' and joined the 'Rhymers' Club', a poets group that was based there.

Davidson was a prolific and hard-working writer. As well as his plays he wrote for the Speaker, the Glasgow Herald, and several other papers. He also wrote and had published several novels and tales, with perhaps the best being 'Perfervid' (1890).

With his reputation gradually providing an income he was also able to explore his true medium; Verse. 'In a Music Hall and Other Poems' (1891) together with 'Fleet Street Eclogues' (1893) were ample proof that he possessed a quite rare, genuine and distinctive poetic gift. Praise came from his peers including George Gissing and WB Yeats who wrote that it was: 'An example of a new writer seeking out new subject matter, new emotions'.

Davidson now turned further and further towards verse. In 1894 he published his most popular volume, 'Ballads and Songs' (1894), and this was followed by a further 'Fleet Street Eclogues' (Second Series) (1896) and by 'New Ballads' (1897) and 'The Last Ballad' (1899).

Davidson was a prolific writer. Besides the works cited, he wrote many other works including, 'The Wonderful Mission of Earl Lavender' (1895), a novel which extends his literary canon to flagellation erotica. He also contributed an introduction to Shakespeare's Sonnets (Renaissance edition, 1908), which, like his various prefaces and essays, shows him to be a subtle literary critic.

As the new century dawned Davidson was hard at work on a series of 'Testaments', in which he gave definite expression to his philosophy and these were published over a seven year period; 'The Testament of a Vivisector' (1901), 'The Testament of a Man Forbid' (1901), 'The Testament of an Empire Builder' (1902), and 'The Testament of John Davidson' (1908).

Though he played down any thought of himself as a philosopher, he expounded an original philosophy which was at once materialistic and aristocratic.

His later verse, which is often fine rhetoric rather than poetry, expressed his belief which is summed up in the last words that he wrote, "Men are the universe become conscious; the simplest man should consider himself too great to be called after any name." Davidson professed to reject all existing philosophies, including that of Nietzsche, as inadequate. The poet planned to expand and expound on his revolutionary creed in a trilogy entitled 'God and Mammon'. Only two plays, however, were written, 'The Triumph of Mammon' (1907) and 'Mammon and his Message' (1908).

In addition to his own work Davidson was a noted translator of other works which included Montesquieu's 'Lettres Persanes' (1892), François Coppée's 'Pour la Couronne' in 1896 and Victor Hugo's 'Ruy Blas' in 1904, the former being produced as, 'For the Crown', at the Lyceum Theatre in 1896, the latter as 'A Queen's Romance' at the Imperial Theatre.

Frank Harris, a member of the Rhymers' Club and himself a writer of erotic literature described him in 1889 as: "... a little below middle height, but strongly built with square shoulders and remarkably fine face and head; the features were almost classically regular, the eyes dark brown and large, the forehead high, the hair and moustache black. His manners were perfectly frank and natural; he met everyone in the same unaffected kindly human way; I never saw a trace in him of snobbishness or incivility. Possibly a great man, I said to myself, certainly a man of genius, for simplicity of manner alone is in England almost a proof of extraordinary endowment."

In 1906 he was awarded a civil list pension of £100 per annum and George Bernard Shaw did what he could to help him financially. However other issues were also circling besides poverty. Ill-health, and his declining intellectual powers, amplified by the onset of cancer, caused profound hopelessness and clinical depression.

Late in 1908, Davidson left London to live in Penzance in Cornwall. On 23rd March 1909, he left his house and was not seen again. There seemed no sound reason not to believe that he had done so with the intention of drowning himself. On an examination of his office a new manuscript was found. It was a poetry book; 'Fleet Street Poems', with a letter bleakly stating confirming, "This will be my last book."

Indeed in his philosophic book 'The Testament of John Davidson', published the year before his death, he anticipates this fate:

"None should outlive his power. . . . Who kills
Himself subdues the conqueror of kings;
Exempt from death is he who takes his life;
My time has come."

Davidson's body was not discovered until 18th September in Mount's cave by some fishermen. In accordance with his will it was now buried at sea. Strangely it seemed Davidson's wish that none of his unpublished works, nor any biography be published and "no word except of my writing is ever to appear in any book of mine as long as the copyright endures."

Davidson's poetry was a key early influence on important Modernist poets, in particular, his compatriot Hugh MacDiarmid, Wallace Stevens and T.S. Eliot.

John Davidson – A Concise Bibliography

The North Wall (1885)
Diabolus Amans (1885) Verse drama
Bruce (1886) A drama in five acts
Smith (1888) A tragedy
An Unhistorical Pastoral, A Romantic Farce (1889)
Scaramouch in Naxos (1889)
Perfervid: The Career of Ninian Jamieson (1890) with 23 Original Illustrations by Harry Furniss
The Great Men, And a Practical Novelist (1891) Illustrated by E. J. Ellis.
In a Music Hall, and other Poems (1891)
Laura Ruthven's Widowhood (with C. J. Wills) (1892)
Fleet Street Eclogues (1893)]
The Knight of the Maypole, (1903)
Sentences and Paragraphs (1893)
Ballads and Songs (1894)
Baptist Lake (1894)
A Random Itinerary (1894)
A Full and True Account of the Wonderful Mission of Earl Lavender (1895)
St. George's Day (1895)
Fleet Street Eclogues (Second Series) (1896)
Miss Armstrong's and Other Circumstances (1896)
The Pilgrimage of Strongsoul and Other Stories (1896)
New Ballads (1897)
Godfrida, a play (1898)
The Last Ballad (1899)
Self's the Man, A tragi-comedy (1901)
The Testament of a Man Forbid (1901)
The Testament of a Vivisector (1901)
The Testament of an Empire Builder (1902)
A Rosary (1903)
The Knight of the Maypole: A Comedy in Four Acts (1903)
The Testament of a Prime Minister (1904) [7]
The Ballad of a Nun (1905)
The Theatrocrat: A Tragic Play of Church and State (1905)
Holiday and other poems, with a note on poetry (1906)
The Triumph of Mammon (1907)

Mammon and His Message (1908)
The Testament of John Davidson (1908)
Fleet Street and other Poems, (1909)
Contributor to The Yellow Book

As Translator

Montesquieu's Lettres Persanes, (Persian Letters) (1892)
François Coppée's Pour la couronne, (For the Crown) (1896)
Victor Hugo's Ruy Blas, (A Queen's Romance) (1904)